FIRST A LONG HESITATION

BOOKS BY EVE SHELNUTT

Eve Shelnutt

First
a
Long
Hesitation

Carnegie Mellon University Press
Pittsburgh 1992

ACKNOWLEDGMENTS

Grateful acknowledgment is due the following journals in which a number of these poems, some in earlier versions, first appeared:

"The Day of Consuelo Gonzales," Oxford Magazine. "Letter From Camaguey, Cuba, 1948," Pig Iron Anthology and New Poets Review. "We Agree," Tamaqua. "Cafe of the Spirits," Poet & Critic. "Taking the Crow to Market," "Where are the Old Fates?" "Alberte November 4, 1987," Nimrod. "O Hero," Chattahooche Review. "Another Burning Boy," America. "The Triumph of Children," North American Review. "One of the Old Men," "I Met You Here Many Times," "At the Edge of Dawn," Prairie Schooner. "The Husband," Black Warrior Review. "Their Mother," "What Will We Do?" Sow's Ear. "A Selected Story," River Styx. "1943," Tar River Poetry. "Father, His Company," "The Adulteress III," "Alphonse," "Are the Lives of the Lovers Altered?" "Proper Travel," Three Rivers Poetry Journal. "Follow Me," Lullwater Review. "Calm, With Gestures," "When Light is Fading,"South Florida Poetry Review. "Collaborators," Apalachee Quarterly. "The Heir," "The Children," Widener Review. "It Seems We Have Returned," Kennesaw Review. "The Adulteress I," Spoon River Quarterly. "The Adulteress II," New Mexico Humanities Review. "Thinking, I Put on My Blue Coat," Art/Life. "Anna, Anna, Anna, Anna," (under the title "Woman Writing at her Desk," Z Miscellaneous.) "Outside the Force of Absolute Mourning," New Delta Review.

Special appreciation is due The Ohio Arts Council for an individual artist's grant; the Yaddo and MacDowell artists colonies for time in residence; and, as always, my husband Mark Shelton, for everything.

Publication of this book is supported by grants from the National Endowment for the Arts in Washington, D.C., a Federal agency, and from the Pennsylvania Council for the Arts.

CONTENTS

V.

VI.

INTERPRETATION

The smell of wool and spices,
of sheep and wood fires
(the wind still blowing),
of boots and leather gloves,
her box of yellow lozenges:
none of it would be easy,
the wounded bird with blood
on its feather, the inaudible
splashing, the disposition of
the hunter, unaccountable happy
and the difference it makes
in the fury coiled inside her.
It will be hard to discover
any scale of values
in their shy irony, then
increasing cheer
as mist lifts, when the girl
she had once been
seems to walk in front of him
erect and yet flexible. But
consider the passage of time,
the instances of matter
lapsing from drama,
and how no child
would put things this way

I.

"*Semblance is wrought over all things.*"
—Zenophanes

THE DAY OF CONSUELO GONZALES

The woman who enjoyed
perfect firmness
is sullied: an illusion
of someone in love.

The doctor will say
what caused her death
while the room weeps
the tallow of candles.

Like a professor
at the end of a lecture
on Don Francho Goya
he will go on talking

while the ones left
go softly away, lax
in the golden afternoon
of fate and tall crosses.

Thus they become
a secret club of two:
the one who spins a rusty tale,
the one who otherwise would listen.

Harsh is the light outside.
Why look at the one who lifts you up?

LETTER FROM CAMAGUEY, CUBA 1948

Our daughter has decided:
tears are a substitute for blood.
Salt mounds her tiny eyes
each with a crow surveying
the incredible distance
and it is perfectly clear
nature has rational patterns,
she the phenomenon varied
only in time and scale.
Believe me, I am learning.

When her eyes are shuttered
but sweetly dreamless
the crows fly to Cayo Pedras
to open the fist of light
in your room where
according to Yolanda's tears
a woman unties your shoes,
licks dust from your swollen lips.
Such efficient courting pleases you
after all these years?

And your denghi fever comes in spurts
when melancholy rains the roof,
when, thinking of us, you glimpse
a unity of design, a pattern
ingrained in serpentine rock.
Sweat pastes the woman's fingers
to your chest and you think:

Is she so poor, so embittered
she *must* be beautiful?
I am turning lovely once again.

Perhaps you should not have sired a daughter
when vengence is time and its savouring.
The crows, I should warn you,
will relate the homology of limbs:
arms of mammals, wings of birds,
and when you return, when her blood
is blood again, you will lean
innocently over her bassinet and lift
the woman Yolanda to your chest
lightly with one hand.

WE AGREE

When Pedro goes with another woman
he brings my father oranges,

my father who once cut sugar cane
in Orizaba until he tasted oranges,

his wounds sliding off to rest
under the curled peel of oranges.

Most things lightly taken, he said,
are hardly worth the trouble

and when one is feeling ruined
almost everything has happened

except the taste of oranges.

CAFE OF THE SPIRITS

I grew weary of songs about hens
and the satisfied fox,
of each torn feather ruffling my throat
until the heart beat exposed
in the moonlight of flesh,
the panting of the fox unbearable.
How the cafe patrons moaned then
waiting. Not a finger
drummed the tables, no woman
touched her hair or rattled bracelets.

I might have become vain
and it is true that mornings
I practiced holding my breath
until even I could feel the fox's teeth
and taste the gush of blood.
To be famous for one note. . . .

It is a bohemian cafe, Love;
I must teach them slowly
though they are restless. Now
in their first nomadic existence
I take them through jagged hills
of what seems like invincible
stone and pray in a minor key:
Let no complications arise!

First they feel cold and begin to cry
as if seized by fits of retching,
the landscape so odd, air scentless.
I hardly breathe, as if song and my body
were brother and sister—an utter calm—
and when the ether wears off, I remember
the slowness of heavy animals,
how their horns grazed my thighs,
birds leaving their nests in formation
screaming against a changing sky.
Pure song: the incredible vertigo.

And so it happens, you appear
toughened by the hard job of becoming a man
entering my skin every night in the same place.

TAKING THE CROW TO MARKET

God knows what a crow
has to do with carrots,
red cabbage, kale
except vanity
fastens its claws to my hair.

Perhaps it imagines me
an inscrutable woman
demanding silence
among figs. Its eyes
in a less domestic setting

might have looked feverish
for a room is dedicated
to its pastimes
and you and I don't pretend
to be man and wife:

two chairs drawn up
before a table;
on a glass-topped stand
a decanter of cut glass;
bread and radishes.

If the crow stares
first at one thing
then another as if its duty
is to preserve a memory
of certain things

I have nothing to say
as it exhales the pungent
odor of oranges: My gluttonous,
my insatiable, my old
voluptuary.

O HERO

His was a house in which the father drank.
So the boy came to have a claim over peaches,
not merely those falling bruised and ready
from trees planted at his birth
but over all the wine not yet made
in tomorow's buzzing,
the knotted cry. Sunlight

at certain hours inflates the downy breasts
of peaches, some orchards from a distance
appear as mounds of children
bored with the game of death.
Patience lies fallow at harvest;
sweet vapors rise from the pickers' bodies
dense with heat. No matter how much they eat
baskets overflow, juice running between wire slats
as though in expiation, without anger,
love. The pits are mute, dazed by light
or a smile of joy. In winter

what then, when the dead draw into anguish
and the living think only of money, masking
their loneliness, what then? He turned away
from this friendly curiosity. And we,
who could find no other outlet for our energy,
waited by the fire, studying our suspect hands.

THEN THE HEAT OF THE SUN

A midsummer's moon stitched to the sky
dropped three memories, or a thousand,
like pesos on the table in the guest house,
its besieged door, and the sound
when it opened of one heart beating
a sea of blood against a thin girl's ribs,
her mouth shaped like a rose, that fragile.

Why wait outside to see if a braver child
returns than the one who entered?
Anyone opening a room of the dead
is the alien element. Women gather
on wooden steps asking one another:
Is your husband in good health?
By chance, nothing more,
the girl will finger wax flowers,
rest her head on the tattered shoulder of a doll.
She might well ask, Where are the people
in the photographs, *is* this a convenient hour?

Now it is years later in a cold climate. Memory
moves an inch to the right, and though
she does not answer the man breathing
love in her ear, she knows she was never
courageous, their house half of brick, half
of nostalgia. Winter afternoons fold
one upon another. Coffins, she remembers,
wait inside a shop she passed daily
in her thin gauze skirt on her way to the cantina
where sugary skulls rest on a shelf.
Christ appears in a tree and says:
Build a chapel for me here.

ANOTHER BURNING BOY

Nada! Nada! Nada! cries the boy
whose basket is empty.
Under trees in the little square,
summer hummed
but not the boy, his arms
heavy with emptiness.

All peace was defiled
by his cry and its echo.
Fruit-sellers kept their daughters
close: to answer denial
was a kind of birth.
Men shook from the seeding.

Nada ! Nada ! Nada !
voluptuous under the sky
until we finally understood.
Then his cry stopped, stopped
at once, even its twin
in the sycamore and smoke.

And the boy held his palms crushed against his eyes.

II.

THE GLASS RELIQUARY

If a word comes to us begging its connotations
the world must answer for the sweet miasma
except the great, inaccessible Ode to Joy.

We should draw lots when our throats rasp
and take turns reading silence to others
who burn to kiss the slothful word.

Fear can be found anywhere and draw us close
as if death had added nothing to its weight
undulating like a mote in thin air.

A trembling past needs freedom, a neutral current
unidentified with any force that struggles.
No questions asked about love, not one.

THE TRIUMPH OF CHILDREN

That man who came down the street
with his brace of women was our father
long before his taming. Who did it
is dead, the marl of their love
forgotten, closeness without intimacy
slippery with our schemes to get out.
Once she tried to rise, to braid our
hair, her earrings icy on our cheeks.
At table we sat with him like cows
half out of a dream or dreamers waking
on their heels. It was the season of
imagination, but not defective. We
let him go. We even tied his shoes.
The whole city seemed to sway like a
cornfield: his Lovelies, and every
romantic aspect of nature. She would
not want to join him looking like that.
Even now, when some figure breaks into
fantasy, I want to translate, to feel
the familiar take on all mystery
in the evening promenade of young men.

ONE OF THE OLD MEN

What would keep us settled
like cooing doves in our paunches
but the advent of disgrace?
To remember our lives
is to imagine only the first, sweet
sip of milk after a bite of bread.
Why did she stay with him? someone asks,
and I see four green doors,
a stamped envelope one night
so quiet you could die without
having heard you had died. And
for no reason we open our mouths
as if we finally understand,
wrapped in rich cloth.
Half-asleep, sleep-walking
a woman named Dolorosa comes to sit
sun-kissed and slender, whom one of us
still wants, noise swelling, a hand
touching her shoulder, shaking her.
She was going to awaken, then stopped.
It has always been like that
in her life, foolish child
unable to forget a sorrow.

MANY TIMES

The most stupid thing would have been
to welcome him among cupboards, white flour, linen:
a woman alone to dress the single bed
or whatever she did with her hands. One man
then another, another, arms, wrists, a waist,
two waists, shoulders and a kind of splendor
when they placed her on a kitchen chair and
broke everything into peculiar shapes to say
legend lived in their breaking. Always
a chicken had to be cooked, or she might have
been kissed, a kiss to taste like dish. But
they never did what they might easily have done—
enough to eat, and walking alone by the seaside
away from the house, the heartstrings, the view
of tapestries. And death creeping into her talk
that she need not hide from another's gaze,
could clearly say *I think of you so often*
and carefully go to bed.

HOUSE OF THE DOLLS

Time quite still in every room
yet they have no other resource,
a kind of education: constant smiles
as their hair wears off in patches.

Still the identical girl will come
with her rigid significance,
a sleeve of sighs,
a bit other-worldly

in her pleated skirt, thick socks,
tender scruples as she looks
daily at their private parts
shaped like a silent mouth.

Who consoles whom? Why ask?
Must they meet on the little
open place before the house,
her delicate neck stretched out?

THE HUSBAND

A little town, its few little houses,
a bandstand peeling in the sun,
the old scribe sitting alone on a bench;
a stand of hemlock; follies, pathos,
pale confusion; a lodger
coming from a church as bells ring,
his tears a sign of spiritual growth;
a bride, much later, descending unattended
in a snow of rice: Have we heard all of this
before? Buy a woman a ticket and you may
never see her. If by determination she comes
she will not be the same who set out that
brilliant Vienna morning: light indescribable,
the cab driver with his amusing lisp,
a juggler practicing on the cobbled street
whom you will never see. But wait, wait
a little in the hush and tension: Love
slides across starched linen like a plate.
Let them talk freely: the bewildered man,
the woman, even the baby dressed in green
with his wondorous babbling. And if
you cherish her image across the table too much,
keep a record of the little town. Ask,
Where is the juggler and How, not quite free,
has he fared?

THEIR MOTHER

Thomas and Vera, the children: asleep
with their hands softly under their cheeks

darkness inaudible around them, mute
tenderness as if they have been answered

or farther away in ancient shadow
beyond the forest of the familiar

they were discovered pulsating there
solid, indifferent, objects of peace.

But the moving obliteration of words
tumble: *duty, the late hour, morning*

voices with their searing little sparks,
the heart with its open door. Then

even the shadows take on a reddish hue
meaning we live among miracles, including

death, and the low whisper of a woman
standing by a bed: "Do not be afraid."

The necessary task. And, turning, they don't
know how the inescapable frightens me

how you can feel the moldering earth
come inside yourself and make a sign.

THE WOMEN

It is their mild orientation to facts
that weighs them down love-defined
as though they were a final warning,
an image drawn from a dream of nature
still unresolved, a dream they pity.
As if to breathe into themselves
a natural distinction, they wash clothes
against stone at a riverside. A
memory of childhood betrayal lives
almost peaceably in them: a just
punishment has been inflicted
but the crime forgotten. What
honor would it be to call them honest?
They have pretty names, and sometimes
lovely bodies, often for years.
They work and say, "I wish you had
seen me then." When they go, presumably
tired of their own cases, they ascend
the stairs together, unlock separate doors.
Lost in thought, Death paces the hall.

OUTSIDE THE FORCE OF ABSOLUTE MOURNING

Eva took to sherry in the afternoon
to smoothe the minute raggedness of time:
spice cakes, creamed dishes, buttery croissants
through the year's parade of couples arriving
and the game of health. One day
it must have come to her, the huntress staying thin,
casting a narrow shadow. Now expectancy quivers
in the air: one season fading, another
rushing in. Sometimes she thinks he has
poured a glass of water and returned to bed
free of fitting the shape of the present.
Its wings grow out of boredom, enclosing her
teasing casualness like parentheses in a set.
The sky seems bare; her heart is almost full.
Through the arch of trees, he watches moon,
stars, clouds, and with bare toes strokes
the long-sleeved winter that she might cross
the dewy grass. Drugged with sugar, what
might she have done? Now, as silent as the rest
who sit wordless— rich, for all he knows, their
forks poised halfway to their mouths— she
wishes him well, and beyond that, under a tree
to an empty table, she is not willing to go.

A SELECTED STORY

Once I went into a cafe
and fell in love so instantly
my head swam with another life.
I was swaying in rose-bright colors
I picked all around me in the fabulous
wide sea as safe as it was warm.
Just such a look. Now
I have got it. And then I could weep
for myself, how I had sometimes done wrong
with breath alone or reckless answers.
I lowered my eyes and huddled
behind a book on Russian history:
the neatly-combed Tsar, trampled earth.
I said to myself I would never weep
again because the black waters of Odessa
are weeping, streaming away. Then
he asked me what I wanted, and that
was the end of our friendship:
two human figures rose in my mind.
And I could not say.

NEIGHBORHOODS

Tonight the lovers next door
pace the wilderness of their room.

We know well this growth
of artificial topiary, these

strange tendrils come upon
by accident. Why

can they not find where they
are going? Suddenly

I remember the boy
selling half a kilo of coffee

across a counter in the Medina,
leaning as though

water rose around his feet.
He helps them still, no doubt:

Hemma, half-deaf Madame Leteef,
the beggar who preferred tea.

With one eye, this boy
almost straddling the island of wood.

Listen to them!
They should go out to buy

little drums for their children
on the Rue Tresor or watch

the girls lining up at the clinic
with their braids straight and still.

I remember how the boy
released himself after work

unsnaking the colored scarves
from his belt, running horse-like

down the cobbled streets.
I went to a window and leaned

far across the sill, I
in my summer dress and sandals.

III.

THIS SPEECHLESS WAIT

It happens in the good homes:
the children's hands
limp as gloves in their laps
until the sound of chewing stops.
Then they must rise and burst
into evening with cries so awkward
loneliness echoes in the dark.
As if they were cattle
who had forgotten grass
even their bodies stop speaking
but for their dangling arms.
Not to be men and women
but projections of their dreams!
In bed comes the wild flight;
refuge: a maw of water
rose-colored, sweet.
They bend carefully over the edge
studying their faces. Morning
is the instant between two fates.
If you open my mouth with yours
we will not rise later and set a table
but let the animals sing.

WHERE ARE THE OLD FATES?

He would have gone to live
in another part of the country
taking his goats and a portrait
over which his sad, melancholy eyes
would flicker as a fire burned.

Or a viper would have bitten him
on the calf and in his delirium
he would have said my name
first with love, then pity
as my mouth drew the poison out.

Instead, he unbuttons my blouse:
From what direction does danger
come to my house if I can do this
and this to your body
where the fever sparkles?

And it would have been too long
an explanation when mist
still lingers on the river.
You must put your arms under your head
and think against a nest of fingers:

If she loves two men without
a thorn in her heart, she would not
want to see them set off together
on the copse on blue horses
with small blue wings.

Now evening has fallen. A sigh
passes through the streets. I have
known these houses for a long time.
Doors open onto many rooms.
We will light every corner with a torch.

PROPER TRAVEL

Not Alva, my mother, alighting
from a subway in Manhattan;
not my father buying a bicycle
during the war; not the absence
of stillness in sirens.

When pleasure stung two shadows
Death came trailing its cane.
Not the spade in the sandpit,
not even two lovely riders weaving
home in the enigma of evening

but a tea party in the kitchen,
children with their tiny cups
and spoons and cubes of sugar.
Where would you like to go, my dear?
Breathing, breathing.

NOW LATE AFTERNOON

We don't want the elephant set adrift
or Wanda sick, making a story short
or the telephone moved from place to place.

We like very much to watch the twins
eating cotton candy on a bench, birds high
in the nameless trees taking the wind.

First of all, of course, we come
to the great river palsying forever
and the city with its steps and the one

face we will never see again.
We don't want to go raving mad for love.
We want to learn to shiver. Yes

two quiet men get up and go away:
a private matter in a room. Why
is a taste of tenderness given us?

1943

You cannot help them, the abrupt declension
of women who have said goodbye to their lovers.
The train will leave on time and, still,
they cannot walk away through narrow streets
where flowerpots designate the bedrooms.
With white-gloved hands raised to their lips
they are for minutes innocent
as their bodies blur in the steaming rumble.
Months later, astride other men, in
new agony, they will notice windows
across the room seeming to open, hear
the familiar cry, *Wait for me*.

FATHER, HIS COMPANY

I meant to ask for money.
    It was Sunday,
day overwhelmed by clouds or,
    floating lost,
the cruel teasing of lovers.
    Alone in the kitchen
he had been eating, or was it
    pure desire
that held a fork to his mouth?
    I thought then
I had a sister who would whisper
    "Rose," "Celia" or "Anne Marie,"
names the fodder of his love.
    The sun was breaking,
my swollen mouth refused.
    And as he chewed his bread
my sister aged, no longer a child,
    and raised her arms.

ALPHONSE

They called his dancing capital;
a man not easily talked down. Still
his face was not applicable to the gift:
bored eyes turning neither left nor right,
detached from superiority, giving nothing
away because—was this it?—
no matter what his feet did he wanted
something from us out of his own reach,
harmless, laughable, almost deferred,
and oh, we tried, our smiles
a delicate task, warmth but not too much,
and at home we wept before falling asleep.

DESIRE

The figures are clothed
far more beautifully
than living men and women.
And the empty beds, their
white counterpanes drawn taut
with no hint of the conjugal,
hours of simply measuring
the distance to a window
while the rest of us
strolled and talked.
In their diaries: the garden
of metaphor, of elegance
to the last detail, and
still a bare spot of expectancy,
a place for the imperative
pursued down stairs,
out onto streets, alone
without anyone beside them,
a kind of union after all.
I mean the same sky,
the outer garments of temperature
and their versions of pleasure
inextricable from pain.

FOLLOW ME

Is my excellent husband faithful?
This silent, anxious brooding!
This vocabulary, fattening. . . .
I list my words

and make sentences of them:
The fair sister whose children
happen to be asleep at the same time:
Krista, a woman of means

the other path of light, a
magnet in the streets. And when
I glance at him, he seems thrilled:
Three days in succession

my fair sister walking with her
parcels like a precious bird.
We are flawed, impertinent
but my heart did not dream

of this happening: the world's bounty
showered on him by nature. I see
the task before me: a little benediction,
words in baskets when my hand is tired

suffering *the rose, the purple asters,*
something hidden in them heavy.
And the sound of bare feet in hallways
inaudible.

VIVE LA JOIE

Who can make every toad princely?
How many notaries fit on a pin's head?
Who pays? Who gets the pretty boy
at a loss to explain his prowess?
The king on his horse and a zig-zag path,
then slowly the brotherly compassion
in the heart of a drunk: who pays?

Clouds are born in the egg of night;
alive is a fine day. The tavernful of
candles and stamping feet has
students reeling against walls with
all they know, creditless. Who sees
the angel change her posture or
water seeping onto the stone floor?

"Once I was looking out the window
of my cell. . . ." And a sparrow circles
each glass more gracefully than dancing.
The two of us once. You came back
sending news that I no longer
belonged to myself. And, oh,
who pays?

CALM, WITH GESTURES

Riders in colored coats on brown mares,
swarthy men something like you
who will not be pushed around; and girls
yes, just beginning to dream of Paris:

stone houses with scant furniture
beautiful from all angles; nature
thick on their walks; and perhaps
an old painter living with his cook.

When that happiness has faded
I would like to stop and talk
awhile, forgetting the usual objects
where they fell. Your house

would be cool, as if the artist
asks, Why not a murmur of darkness
for a woman who has walked
in fearing so little?

It is all indefinite now, even where
to look. How exhausted they are:
sweat-stained horses, everywhere
the smell of patchouli, men at draughts,

so many painters piling into
a single city. I would discover you
in the bow of a little boat,
rowing the downy neck of afternoon.

WATCHING

This morning my husband
younger than I by years
took off across a field
to grieve for his father
dying under memory's ash.
Every morning for a week
we have put fresh flowers
in a vase on the table.
Outside wild fowl flew past
watchful and sqawking.
He walked near a fence
to empty himself of a poison
or the imagined eruptions
of heaven
and that was all except
as he turned back
a tremor went through me.

LUCK IN WINTER

With her crumpled knee
who could stand her
limping to swine and cattle
with their sentimental names,
stutter of poetry gnawing
at their ears, then:
crisp snap of fingers?
The lucky are just so many,
never the same, sprinkling
crumbs on the steeple-tip
of time. Sometimes
a wooden spoon
is found beside a rock.
Who could stand her
adjusted walk pale and damp
like a worm through wood?
Which knee would you
squeeze briskly into likelihood?
She doesn't care: grass
has begun to listen, a
privet hedge divides the field,
fragrance blooms her skirt
and oh the Noisy One is coming
to shatter the water.

IV.

WHEN LIGHT IS FADING

Have I taken something from the air
as a kitchen girl after work
will gasp in the orchard
awaiting the end of waiting,
the world so full of apples,
the mutilation of apples?

Who can suffer bravely the lore
of women rolling crusts, men's deeds
flung like scraps against a wall
as the dogs snarl wordlessly
doomed to hunger? The women
suppose she knows nothing.

Have we not had enough of calamity,
that knife scarring our hands,
peels curled on the tiles,
the wailing children? Have you
cleaned a table after an old woman
has eaten? Trust me

I who know the human howl over plates
would do nothing shocking.
Notice how the apples hang lightly
by their stems. Calmly I would touch
the knowledge of your body
gathering the tumult in.

FIRST A LONG HESITATION

For nine years I waited at a window
while you gathered your belongings
and moved toward me, polite enough
when I opened the door not to mention
where you had been, why I should have known
you were coming, though those who are gone
leave a place waiting for them, even
the dead. Forgive me if I love the short hour
before dawn when birds waken from the vapor
of cold leaves. Alberte, a few doors away,
will rise soon to send curls of smoke
into the sky like a sad voice, a dialect
I waited for: any sound over my head
filling the holes. And if Alberte died,
I told myself, then it would be better
to look for the river's curve into oblivion
where I was born and could find my tears.
To display what I owned wrapped in flesh,
a globe of the world in my head:
had I counted on it in the map of my heart?

WHEN

When soft strange ventriloquisms
come from holes in the ground
what keeps a screen between us
and despair? It is not a matter
of theology or innocence
but the words we see
when we see each other:
dry, warm, unconscious of travel
thinking once of love
think of it again, not like
the erratic beast choking
on death's bone but a crack
in the meadow widening
into the sky's clear blue,
the artifice of mind.
When I think of you
and see you
you are the same one.

I MET YOU HERE MANY TIMES

Music
and tables where men could sit
slowly drinking wine
in the violet tint of winter
drawn without delineation,
untroubling. White napkins
over their knees as though
they had chosen this hour
for a ceremony honoring
the mastery of grief.
Three smoked cigarettes
to dispose of time, humane
and gentle, almost. Not a siren,
no sound but glass on marble,
the guitar of the Italian
earning money probably half-relieved
by the solitude of the room,
after a lifetime of rooms.
Shhhh. Even where you sat, the wind
stung. And you didn't see
how we could go, at once go,
leaving them.

COLLABORATORS

Were we naive to talk across a table?
The ice broke, quickened, and I went under
as you watched me enter a region known for its beauty
though only we had gone there, each alone, alone
as a tenor singing an aria on the radio
or your father drumming on a pane of glass:
something hurts him and yet sometimes he is happy—
a remembered lime tree giving off the scent of a woman
or schoolgirls carrying prayer books in their arms.

The tenor? His breath has warmed the water.
This might well be Italy, its serious black,
and I want to live in a district so remote
we put aside our taste for the perfect dwelling:
a boathouse, incautious scenery bewitching.
Remember: I did not once shudder or open my mouth
to the coarse expression of drowning
though sweet is the image of drowned and perished beauty.

I would love your father if I could.

THE HEIR

With his sister he stands at a window
glazed by early light and on the other side
by their mother's tears luminous
as the eyes of foxes
when what they fear is dazzling.

Between the light of the father's leaving
and the woman who will stay put, so stunned,
the boy waves because he cannot help it,
such is his freedom. I know it
from this distance when, yesterday,

he touched me for the first time,
his arms flying up to say
wait, wait, it will enter you.

IN A TOLERANT AGE

You meant disgrace that went deep,
rising each morning with my body
like the smells of pride and sorrow
of our occupation in strange rooms
dispossessed and inquisitive. You meant
not the place where we first
touched each other shyly
but the cool appraisal of reality
indifferent to a final answer. Yes
you entered the wound you opened
saying no word, not putting on the light.
Only the eruption gave proof, only
the proof awakened me to shame.

THE STILL DESIRE

Her red jacket on a chair,
the last light transformed,
a foam of light cresting into evening.

To tiptoe, to keep quiet . . .
But rain would also serve:
subtle differences in the nervousness

of night, and crumpled images
as if red shoes, too, had been tossed
beneath the chair. Nameless:

the reality accumulating
more and more triumphant despite
silence, whatever light or rustling.

This word, these syllables: *Anna*
for whom the hour of giving has struck,
her face illumined and naked

her whole body shivering, and
white gloves for going away
paired neatly on the table:

What did I tell you? And her cry
when you entered her, one sharp cry
splitting the world in two.

IT SEEMS WE HAVE RETURNED

Invisible lives in darkness,
hammocks filled in season
with flowers or ice. Sparse mercies
whose time of mutation has not come.
The shadowy time of vines,
of the spreading stain
of the eyes of animals
listening to the shifting earth,
to the golden foot of fire dragging close
when all will be stricken by invention:
adventure beginning, and misery.
Here, then, is our celebration: a tableau
of a couple dancing, nothing
warming our waxen backs, skin
trembling in the last motion all its own,
featureless faces turned toward
the promise of mystery,
no one stepping from a lighted portico
across the distance of a compass,
no agony of the sailor. No place for him,
not yet.

"WHAT WILL WE DO?"

We will go to a country
where it is necessary to buy light:
an ember on a drop of oil,
a candle from a priest, or Amar
counting our notes saying
"You are not so poor."

There bells ring at dusk,
each reverberation a symbol
of forgotten pain. Heat a shawl
of emotion we cannot name.
The air's fine grit scours the floor
of a tiny shop selling silk

an element so rich we absorb
a surfeit of time woven into camels
who never thirst. *Do you have*
a memory of childhood engraved
so deeply you cannot conceive
of life without it?

The particular alley is like that,
the door you open when you come
tired from labor that buys us light.
Some nights you are so weary
you plant a solemn kiss on my forehead
and we sleep turned from one another.

Mornings the sun dazzles us,
the women's tales are credible.
At the edge of the sea the freighter
slips finally into darkness. How sad
the passengers' voices lifting like gulls:
What will we do, what will we do?

WAITING

I have not cried
but stood in the same place
for a long time, expecting
something to push me
into another world.

It is a kind of birth,
the creature writhing
from its ill-fitting sheath.
I don't know why
when one animal wails

all of them answer.
If someone comes to you
after years and years
to put his hand
on your shoulder

you will continue
as though you had rested
for an hour at dawn
waking startled by the voices
of all sheep

in the one struggling to stand.

THE VISIT

After hours of rain falling
sometimes in the rhythm of a gait
the house is still again

but for the door rattling its hook:
a residue or promise. Suppose
I had a jealous husband

and all he could remember
was the look of a room: the chairs,
the calendar? If he simply *was*

and waited? Last night I felt his desperation.
The sensual seemed for the first time
to have an honorable place. I mean

simply alive, the difference between life
and life conceived as a story:
A woman loves a blacksmith and runs daily

from her house to the sound of bellows,
to the slightest smoke rising. And a boy,
observing, tells their story puzzled

maybe making a startled sound
when the blacksmith finally touches her—
something the boy isn't, would never be:

a man making love while a boy is watching.
The boy's story, you see. And for so long
I didn't know whether you and I were

a vision of two lovers being watched,
no whisper rising from us. And no breaking.
And my house when rain fell on it

how desolate it was!
I love you more than I knew.

EVENING TALES

I.

At this hour I believe
I am conscious of your body.

The wind dies, the town dozes;
we listen to wild dogs

barking in the distance.
And calmly you say

you will see our fate, whatever
it is, through to the end.

But something worse than fire begins:
the Past waking to my silence.

Always I am startled by its courage
as men walk in single file

saying all they can remember,
increasing animation like people

talking at random to ease themselves
of a concept, maybe sweetness

or the need to pretend. So they would
engage me forever. It's then

you raise you bright boy-eyes
and ask once more

if you may come to my room
in the morning.

We are two people alone. Then
guided by voices I walk down the path.

II.

I seem to have entered a room
and found another woman's life inside.

She has pleasure to give
on the clean, white sheets.

Yes the best hour is morning
when light begins to show

between cracks in the shutters,
fine weather holding.

I have been awake and restless
for so long.

III.

Now let us pray against evening
without daring to stop

for they were not mere intruders
but the Dead flushed from hiding.

Their discussions threaten to begin
as if we must know not love

but the ceaseless nature of suffering.
Anything they say helps them

pass the time after so much looking.
The settling sun throws every detail

into relief. Ask God why
a rapport exists between naked bodies

fields washed in light, and the moon
fat and embarrassed and ashamed.

THE ADULTERESS

I.

He let me sleep in a wooden house by the sea,
light flowing like water in a gutter along the hall.
The smell of salt, screech of birds crying "shame!"
were meant to purge my blood, but my husband waited
like a saint with broken legs who knows rebuke
can be a kiss, a scent of jasmine, the shiver
of twigs along a path. Nights I saw you gesture
at the sky. Your mouth opened as though you were
shouting. The gray sky lightened, weak and exhausted
as wind blew on the tiny flame of sun. Where
had it begun against common sense? The air was silk,
swelling. And you began to speak our language,
unsated thought, slowly. I held to the rim of the sea
with each stoke feeling a wave of faintness
and my heart's knocking. No, I will never return to water.
Yes, my eyes are open like a fish who has relinquished hope.
And is this, Love, what you wanted, the strangeness of it
with me forever, my husband struggling each morning to walk?

II.

Because we love one another
the dead enter our room
crowding like cattle around a trough of hay.
Always they assemble to our breathing.
Even their bells are still as I say your name.
A small town on the Prusso-Slavic plain: gone.
Gone, the night of the giraffe, faded silk,
blowing hair, the reflections of a shadow.
Tolerant of innumerable treacheries,
they did not want to have memory killed,
flat pangs of consciousness taken away.
It is good of them to have come, our room
having been viewed already, and forgotten,
our riches, not our crimes, stirring them to awe.

III.

I am careful with your name
taken from our room among strangers,
those good illiterate women
with little girls hidden inside them
liking pleasures they will not admit.
Or men whose painful concentration
shows only in the act of love.
I feel they will hear nostalgia in it
but for that there is no word: always
the same, stretched across the horizon.
Once I saw a boy tie the legs and tail
of a mosquito, letting it settle on him
in peace. The point of view local,
precise. Evening, the Hour of the Mosquito.
In a million years the boy will explain
everything, his eyes a bare esplanade of
tranquility. So clemency comes with
the silent witness of images? Tonight
I sat among others for a long time without
talking and at first my silence puzzled them:
a fish who has swallowed the river.
Then they heard water closing over your body.
Someone swimming in darkness. What
was he waiting for? Why didn't he take her away?

THE CHILDREN

The children
have followed you
up a hill. Not your own
who lack nothing

but my emissaries whose births
were never registered
nor baptisms nor confirmations
as if it is not clear

that they are strong enough
to bear this life
of following you
with an invitation

inscribed like a stigmata
on their open palms,
except you have compassion
for all children

and turning to the sound
of familiar song
you notice the girls' socks
slipping below their knees

the boys' short ties askew.
You will stop. It is
the habit of your hands
as if disorder

in a child's clothing
were a kind of weeping
no matter how sweetly
he sings.

I know, of course,
the crime of sending children
on such a mission
but they live with me.

One night the youngest
whose eyes are so like yours
observed by chance
Death making an opening

so terrible
it was he who spoke to the others
of contagion, ending where?
You could say

they come for themselves.
But when you stop
to smoothe their hair
or offer chocolates

read their palms:
I am the Empress of Air.
You see how it delights them,
how the dance they imagine

is the cure?

LISTENING FOR THE SOUND

No one has seen me go near you for weeks.
Each hour has been like a room where a woman
stands turning before a mirror in the light
of a single lamp. She might brush her hair
endlessly except, outside, the frozen fields
are conferring in a circle as the blank
countryside moves past. They are drawn
to the odor of musk as if to ask
whether everything has not lost its intimacy
numb with cold. It is natural for them
to move slowly toward the light pink
in the late hour and press against the glass.
What if she began to cry, began to choke
on her tears, and they rushed down the hall
opening the door to make her stop? Or
if a porter carrying your bags up a hill
could see no end to hills? If you heard her say
Goodnight, logs in the fireplace breaking in two?
If you heard her notebook open, the pen scratching,
and knew when you found her you would read
every word she had written?

IN YOUR ABSENCE

How desperate the trees have become
as if no one had troubled that calmer green
by seeing and hearing, thinking or knowing:
the common mistake. And now the wind
takes gaudy offerings to the dead
startled among gravestone thick with disgust.

Lovers in half-light, shadow of thought:
we will be forgiven when the great crimes
are counted. Listen to me:
that morning when I was crying, I almost
awakened you with shuddering desire.
The barbarism of decay held me back.

Passion can so easily turn morbid,
and it frightened me: the red quilt,
the dream of your father as a boy in a white dress
holding out a cup of wine. Soon, as he knows,
the politeness of November will come.
Then the immaculate vengence of time.

THINKING, I PUT ON MY BLUE COAT

I will walk by the Waters of Loneliness
leading the angel away in her amazing body
and the rest will be so simple: an hour, say,
of sentience if she will sit calmly on a bench
as we have coffee, cake, your fingers
on my face, *so much mine*, among the crowd
until we are restored, after which you may
ask her to dance the hard-won-heaven tango.
I wouldn't mind then.

V.

ALBERTE, NOVEMBER 4, 1987

The configuration of the land
into a row of small black buggies
and a tree hooked on a rock:
the connection had to be made
by waiting.
A red stain on leaves or on a bed
that never owned a man:
Who jumps in with reasons, saying
"Ah!" and looks off at a rise
as if a house were built there
already? Not what he loves
but what is coming in the air, as if
to see is a thing he does not know.
There was a closet where her hat hung
and the living sympathies of her hands
in the vase of hydrangea on a table.
Strangers passing her gate daily
proclaiming admiration for each other
in their bows. When she died
it was not that the tree
moved away from the rock
but that it seemed to move.

ARE THE LIVES OF THE LOVERS ALTERED?

Nothing anyone could write
would disclose the meaning
of a year's unfolding
in Alberte's intelligent face.
Anna's experience was in the nature
of the room itself,
the effect of Alberte's death
only seeming, as we know,
to depend on an odor.
In Anna's letter of 4 November 1987
the handling of detail is confused,
the vase an awkward symbol
holding the details together
for a long journey. It is true
that every love story
depends pathetically on coincidence:
that he and she happen to meet.
Consider the phrase *lucky in love*.
How easily, somewhere, at a specific time,
he might have missed her. In this instance,
however much we may feel, a flaw
exists in the necessity itself
for Anna's letters. Or, perhaps
better said, in the young man's belief,
days after Anna has ceased crying,
that the odor of hydrangea envelopes him.

NATURE, ONE MIGHT SAY

A man with emerald birds for hair.
A man with emerald birds for hair
reading a book engraved in metal,
a large world hidden behind those words.
How dignified he is, how austere
in his thinking. I want
to throw my head back, ask, Is this
a madhouse, all things just as your please?
We unpack the heroic virtues, say
"Sleep well" and, turning, recite
the words of parting: *safe, safe.* It's
definite: We shall not see one another
again. Yet all my life
I have liked listening for something
that doesn't like to make a sound.
To possess the fabulous goods: the wheels,
the gleaming doorknobs, to watch them
shiver under my hands into silence. . . .
Notice: Everything seems to be
asleep, even the horses graceful
and dense. I walk quickly
past the tall houses smothered in dusk.
If I made him a present of all adornments
so he would never look into a mirror,
could he sleep garlanded by my breathing?

SIGNIFICANCE WILL MOVE AGAIN

Significance will move again
across the gray-blue of his eyes.
The rough cloth of meaning
will polish his memory like a gem.
Suddenly the pose of a listener
will be his, as dramatic as snow,
truth covering the old arrogance
until its shape is rounded beautifully
in ways not quite clear to him
but interesting: What a lover
he has taken on! Expectation
will exceed his passion and become
itself a passion such as the
knife-thrower's wife must feel.
It will be late, every pair of eyes
turned toward the door, even the
petals of Spring late in their falling.
By pure chance, will you be there
open, pure as sunlight, every branch?
Some silence can be deafening
in this kind of landscape. But
there's an order slow in its movement
clearing glasses from the table
for the young have no shame about time.

Come in, come in, sit
like all the years of my life.

VI.

ANNA, ANNA, ANNA, ANNA

He knows she will read his letter with her elbows
placed resolutely on the table.
And he has thought of her for a long time,
of the difficulty of approach, like the lover
who paradoxically loves virginity. So it turns out
he does not want to risk being patronized
because there is grace in the world
though he never expects to receive it.
What we do now, he added, is neatly kept
but very poor, a dumb anguish. I have never
been good at finding words, knowing well
why things happen. Here where visitors
rarely come, I have got back my sight
and everything seems to tell me what it signifies.
You would laugh, send me to buy black clothes.
But the essence of my nature is longing.

And he never knew what went on inside her,
the one who went in and out of a house comprehending
how easy it is to take a naked man in your arms.

ASSUMING ALL GOES WELL GOD WILL SAY

How do you know he loved you
when he touched you, what?
a dozen times? And
you didn't think he loved you
only then. It was as if
you'd been struck for all
of what you call time. But
women can watch a world
they never made
and estimate forces of which
they've only heard. Why
did he write to you so
infrequently? Since he loved you
it is interesting to consider.
One day (you wouldn't know this)
he bent mysteriously
over the ground for minutes
as if to be bent double
was what he had expected.
He went on quietly afterwards.
Well let it be. When you confess
I may or may not pity you.

AT THE EDGE OF DAWN

This man,
I thought he had seen me before,
had formed an opinion of my
estrangement from nature and all
applause, and now our swindle
would begin with just so much
money for coffee, trouble worn out
and conversation about the old
Berlin to raise our spirits.
We were in the world and sometimes
sorry. I thought heaven had vanished
and with it the childish wail and
plans and the attraction of fate.
I believed our words informed us
of their sadness; that we could bring
flowers to one another like two cats
sharing their mauled birds. I thought
his first gesture would cause a curtain
to fall over the illness of ourselves,
and it would be best to be walking home
trembling imperceptibly to the
soul's habitual roar, that my ancestors
would be pleased, still hold me in favor,
with radiant nonsense swept away. I thought
he thought as I did, and we could take
as much time as we liked saying goodbye.

Carnegie Mellon Poetry

1982
The Granary, Kim R. Stafford
Calling the Dead, C.G. Hanzlicek
Dreams Before Sleep, T. Alan Broughton
Sorting It Out, Anne S. Perlman
Love Is Not a Consolation; It Is a Light, Primus St. John

1983
The Going Under of the Evening Land, Mekeel McBride
Museum, Rita Dove
Air and Salt, Eve Shelnutt
Nightseasons, Peter Cooley

1984
Falling from Stardom, Jonathan Holden
Miracle Mile, Ed Ochester
Girlfriends and Wives, Robert Wallace
Earthly Purposes, Jay Meek
Not Dancing, Stephen Dunn
The Man in the Middle, Gregory Djanikian
A Heart Out of This World, David James
All You Have in Common, Dara Wier

1985
Smoke from the Fires, Michael Dennis Browne
Full of Lust and Good Usage, Stephen Dunn (2nd edition)
Far and Away, Mark Jarman
Anniversary of the Air, Michael Waters
To the House Ghost, Paula Rankin
Midwinter Transport, Anne Bromley

1986
Seals in the Inner Harbor, Brendan Galvin
Thomas and Beulah, Rita Dove
Further Adventures With You, C.D. Wright
Fifteen to Infinity, Ruth Fainlight
False Statements, Jim Hall
When There Are No Secrets, C.G. Hanzlicek

1987
Some Gangster Pain, Gillian Conoley
Other Children, Lawrence Raab
Internal Geography, Richard Harteis
The Van Gogh Notebook, Peter Cooley
A Circus of Needs, Stephen Dunn (2nd edition)
Ruined Cities, Vern Rutsala

Places and Stories, Kim R. Stafford

1988
Preparing to Be Happy, T. Alan Broughton
Red Letter Days, Mekeel McBride
The Abandoned Country, Thomas Rabbitt
The Book of Knowledge, Dara Wier
Changing the Name to Ochester, Ed Ochester
Weaving the Sheets, Judith Root

1989
Recital in a Private Home, Eve Shelnutt
A Walled Garden, Michael Cuddihy
The Age of Krypton, Carol J. Pierman
Land That Wasn't Ours, David Keller
Stations, Jay Meek
The Common Summer: New and Selected Poems, Robert Wallace
The Burden Lifters, Michael Waters
Falling Deeply into America, Gregory Djanikian
Entry in an Unknown Hand, Franz Wright

1990
Why the River Disappears, Marcia Southwick
Staying Up For Love, Leslie Adrienne Miller
Dreamer, Primus St. John

1991
Permanent Change, John Skoyles
Clackamas, Gary Gildner
Tall Stranger, Gillian Conoley
The Gathering of My Name, Cornelius Eady
A Dog in the Lifeboat, Joyce Peseroff
Raised Underground, Renate Wood
Divorce: A Romance, Paula Rankin

1992
Modern Ocean, James Harms
The Astonished Hours, Peter Cooley
You Won't Remember This, Michael Dennis Browne
Twenty Colors, Elizabeth Kirschner
First A Long Hesitation, Eve Shelnutt
Bountiful, Michael Waters
Blue for the Plough, Dara Wier
All That Heat in a Cold Sky, Elizabeth Libbey